YOUR KNOWLEDGE HAS V.

Aria Reid

Irish Travellers' Shelta - A Future Language or a Future for the Language

GRIN Verlag

Bibliografische Information der Deutschen Nationalbibliothek:

Die Deutsche Bibliothek verzeichnet diese Publikation in der Deutschen National-
bibliografie; detaillierte bibliografische Daten sind im Internet über http://dnb.d-
nb.de/ abrufbar.

Imprint:

Copyright © 2011 GRIN Verlag GmbH
Druck und Bindung: Books on Demand GmbH, Norderstedt Germany
ISBN: 978-3-656-39244-6

This book at GRIN:

http://www.grin.com/en/e-book/210261/irish-travellers-shelta-a-future-language-
or-a-future-for-the-language

GRIN - Your knowledge has value

Der GRIN Verlag publiziert seit 1998 wissenschaftliche Arbeiten von Studenten, Hochschullehrern und anderen Akademikern als eBook und gedrucktes Buch. Die Verlagswebsite www.grin.com ist die ideale Plattform zur Veröffentlichung von Hausarbeiten, Abschlussarbeiten, wissenschaftlichen Aufsätzen, Dissertationen und Fachbüchern.

Visit us on the internet:

http://www.grin.com/

http://www.facebook.com/grincom

http://www.twitter.com/grin_com

Modularbeit

Irish Travellers' Shelta

-

A Future Language or a Future for the Language

List of contents

1. Introduction

Around 86.000 Irish Travellers live all over the world and define themselves by an unusual and unique lifestyle. They see themselves as a distinct ethnic group that lives within settled society. This view is underlined by a language that is only spoken amongst the members of the travelling community. Shelta – a language which strongly withholds the grip of linguistic researchers until today and which also protects its speakers and the community's identity from non-acceptance and feelings of inferiority. In advance I have to make clear that many – though interesting – but conflicting assumptions have been made on Irish Travellers and have yet to be proven. Not only more research has to be done in order to discover the roots of Travellers and their language, but also a way has to be found to make it possible for Irish Travellers to feel like a part of the society they live in. In my paper I will briefly introduce the most important issues on Irish Travellers, go more into detail concerning the use and the structure of Shelta, and discuss the assumptions on its origin and value.

2. Irish Travellers

2.1 Origin and history

"Nomadism [...] means little or no traces left of one's passing." (Sinéad Ní Shúinéar 1994, 60)

The origin and background of Irish Travellers is very vague and after more than a century of research still raises a lot of questions. The terms 'tinkler', 'tinker' or 'tynker' are probably the oldest names for Travellers. It derives from their occupation as tradespeople and craftworkers. Although "By 1175, 'tinkler' and 'tynker' began appearing in records as trade or surnames" (G. Gmelch and S.B. Gmelch 1976, 227), the description of nomadic traders has already been mentioned in pre-Christian writings. Sources from around the 1500s show the existence of Travellers in great parts of Ireland and Scotland.[1] According to references from earlier centuries it seems like Irish Travellers have somehow always existed. Nevertheless, their presence has been noticed more often in times of plight and disaster – for instance during the Irish Famine. The Travellers fled, came out on the streets in multitudes, and due to their nomadic lifestyle and unsettledness became outlaws of society. They were disparaged by the settled communities. There are few relevant sources to reconstruct the history of Irish Travellers and therefore no possibility to estimate their true origin.[2] Nonetheless, there are many contentious theories about their origin. Some of these derive from their language Shelta as it is closely related to Old Irish and English. Sinéad Ní Shúinéar proposes three hypotheses that seem to be the most reasonable ones to consider when dealing with the origin of Irish Travellers. The first hypothesis assumes that the Irish Travellers are descended from a pre-Celtic group. Hence they lived in Ireland before the arrival of the Celts and were oppressed by its invaders. If they had a nomadic lifestyle at the time of the invasion is unknown. The second hypothesis states that Travellers are the descendants of one of several distinct Celtic groups which took part in the invasion of Ireland. And finally, according to the third hypothesis the Irish Travellers descend from indigenous nomadic craftsmen who were independent from, a sub-group within or derived from the Celtic invaders.[3] Nonetheless, it is unknown whether the Irish Travellers became a sub-group voluntarily or were forced to leave Ireland by the Celtic invaders. Beginning with the Great Irish Famine (1845-1852) and the Highland Clearances (18th & 19th century) thousands of people fled the country due to mass starvation and expulsion of the Gaels during that time. Immigrants and amongst them Irish Travellers left the country on the 'coffin' ships to the new world. There they have not been recognized as a unique ethnic group yet. Since they have always lived with a high level of secrecy the population of Travellers in the U.S. can only be estimated. Hence the numbers reach from approximately 10.000 to 40.000 Travellers in the States. Irish Travellers are mostly located in the Southern States of the U.S. like Ala-

---

[1] G. Gmelch and S.B. Gmelch, The Emergence of an Ethnic Group: The Irish Tinkers (Anthropological Quarterly, 1976) 227.
[2] S.Ó Síocháin, J. Ruane, M. McCann, Irish Travellers: Culture and Ethnicity. (Belfast, W&G Baird Ldt. 1994) xiii.
[3] S. Ní Shúinéar, Irish Travellers: Culture and Ethnicity. (Belfast, W&G Baird Ldt. 1994) 70.

bama, Mississippi, Texas and South Carolina but are also found in the areas around Ohio. Since Travellers live a nomadic life they travel all around the country to do handiwork during the warmer seasons and return to their residences in the winter like migratory birds.

To settled society and undoubtedly a great deal of researchers the existence and lifestyle of Travellers is a very interesting and important phenomenon which makes it more unbelievable to them that "Travellers everywhere are supremely indifferent to their own origins." (Sinéad Ní Shúinéar 1994, 60) The secretive lifestyle of Irish Travellers has protected their culture and history as best as it could until today and will probably still raise a lot of questions in further anthropological, historical and linguistic research.

2.2 Culture and Ethnicity

"You have to be born a Traveller, you cannot become one." (McCarthy 1994, 124)

Irish Travellers have a distinct and valuable culture with an own history and development and therefore see themselves as a unique ethnic group. An ethnic group is by definition a group of human individuals who share a common culture, religion, heritage and language or dialect. Mostly ethnic groups are minorities in a larger society.[4] "Ethnicity is not just a matter of personal choice" (O'Connell 1994, 110) but of roots, history and tradition that is passed on from generation to generation.

Irish Travellers have enclosed their culture from the settled society throughout the centuries through language, endogamy and cultural differences. Tinkers differentiate between two worlds – namely Travellers and non-Travellers. Travellers are nomads and "First and most obvious, nomadism means a material culture pared down to the portable minimum" (Sinéad Ní Shúinéar 1994, 60). The possibility to travel at all times and by all means is fundamental to the existence of Travellers. They are always on the move and therefore only own be-

---

[4] A.S. Hornby, et al., eds, <u>Oxford Advanced Learner's Dictionary of Current English</u>. (Oxford, Oxford Univ. Press, 2000) 424.

longings they can take on their journeys. Consequently transport is an important issue in the life of a Traveller and most of their salary goes into the funding of their need to stay mobile. This lifestyle enables them to great independence and flexibility in means of economic adaption. Through that their flexibility they are able to adapt more easily to changes and different working situations. They are mostly in favor of self-employment and have a strong feeling against wage labor since it imposes a restriction to their lifestyle.

Also family plays a central and dominant role in the life of a Traveller. Their family system is defined by a dense patriarchal family structure and is composed of small closed groups of extended families. These stand for company, support and give the members a feeling of safety since they are still regarded and disliked in today's society. Also the elderly are highly respected because they are the bearers of traditions (mostly oral) and wisdom which includes the knowledge and the transmission of cleansing and death rituals. Furthermore Irish Travellers live almost entirely endogamous. Arranged marriage within the community is very common and supports the issue of secrecy amongst the Traveller societies. One could wonder if that fact might not have led to extinction because of incest causing hereditary diseases over a long period of time. Though this is also a very controversial issue amongst researchers it serves the importance of distinction. "Travellers are physically distinct from the settled society" (Ní Shúinéar 1994, 55) and "Genetic studies corroborate this popular perception by confirming differentiation between the Traveller und settled Irish populations." (Ní Shúinéar 1994, 55) In conclusion one could therefore say regarding the issue of secrecy that Irish Travellers are biologically self-reproducing to tighten the bonds between the already close knit communities.

Furthermore and very unfortunately a lot of the Traveller traditions have been lost due to oppression and feelings of shame for their own lifestyle. Also illiteracy is a big issue amongst Irish Travellers and only sharpens the negative attitude members of the settled society have towards them. In spite of all the obvious differences and the 'fulfilled' criteria for being an ethnic group a lot of people do not accept Travellers as such. But what we should actually all agree on is that there are the least parallels between the culture of the Travellers and those of any settled community worldwide. Therefore Patricia McCarthy points out correctly that the "Traveller culture is not a sub-culture but a culture in its own right" (McCarthy 1994, 123).

Owning to all these facts stated it is extremely difficult for Travellers to assimilate to the lifestyle of the settled society. Nevertheless they want to be accepted and valued by outside society and to be seen as individuals with an identity of their own. Non-Travellers seem to fear the travelling communities because of their differences in lifestyle. This problem is mainly caused by their ignorance towards Irish Travellers and results from the secrecy with which the latter treats their lives. Nevertheless the misunderstanding and fear needs to be replaced by an open-minded perception of difference in order to see Irish Travellers for who they really are. Without that acceptance Irish Travellers will go on hiding their culture and language from the surrounding society causing a never ending circle of mistrust and ignorance for each other.

3. Travellers 'Secret' Language

3.1 The use of Shelta

The term Shelta for Traveller language is normally not used by its speakers but has become the academic term for their language and covers the spoken varieties of the Traveller groups Gammon and Cant. Travellers do not at all reflect on their use of language but see it merely as a tool to keep their lives distinct from the settled society.

In the 1880s the first written assumptions on the Travellers language were published with an interesting explanation for the different language. Linguists assumed that according to Travellers professions Shelta was a secret language used by the occupational group to exclude outsiders from their field of work. The conclusion drawn from that information is that in the 1880s Irish Travellers were not regarded as an ethnic minority but a group of people within their society that distinguished itself through a dialect or jargon like other occupational groups such as lawyers, scientists or doctors. Nowadays we know that Irish Travellers are "a natural social group" (Binchy, 11) with an own language hardly touchable by outsiders of the community as well as a distinct and valuable culture with an own history and development. The problem that occurs when trying to arouse interest for the language it is taken as seriously as their speakers – namely not at all. The knowledge on the language that settled society has only reflects what they think of Travellers. To them it is a poor imitation, a hotchpotch of Irish and English without an own grammatical structure and a complexity recognized languages have. Shelta is a language with a reduced function in terms of structure and use.

Therefore one might wonder why Shelta lacks these linguistic features and has not been able to establish a complex speech system. On the other hand one should ask if those features are absolutely necessary for communication and for the definition of a language. Regarding the lifestyle of the travelling community and its tight relationships it becomes more obvious that Shelta might not need such a complexity. Dense, small enlarged family groups do not have the need for a complex language. Shelta does not serve Travellers to communicate in the way settled society does in situation based communication but to connect secretly through the language that has constantly survived centuries. It is all about the message that has to be conveyed, the bare information that is used to "get things done" (Binchy 1994, 146) and to signal membership to the group. It is in such means a secret language that it is only used amongst Travellers. The message the language conveys is not exclusively secret but private between Travellers. If Shelta is at all used in the presence of outsiders it is larded with few English words so that the cursorily listener will not realize that a different language is spoken. The use of the non-Traveller language only occurs in necessary contact situations. Often outsiders have difficulties understanding Travellers when they speak their simplified version of this language. "Traveller English is a cohesive and distinctive entity [regardless of geography] because of its Gammon underlay." (Ní Shúinéar 1994, 58)

When it comes to the use and function of Shelta similarities to pidgin and creole can be drawn. Pidgin and Shelta are in so far comparable that they share the need for communication within their community, the need to create a safe environment excluding outsiders. With pidgin, communication is "stripped of all but the barest necessities" (Binchy 1994, 144). That basically means the social messages that language conveys through grammar and style is redundant. In some ways this is also true for Shelta. Nevertheless Shelta is different in the sense that it is shared between people with the same background and not like pidgin formed to communicate between different foreign backgrounds in order to have a common language. Also unlike pidgin which develops into a creole language after the next generation is born, Shelta has not changed and developed over the centuries due to the Travellers social position. Thus Shelta could not spread into other contexts of use what prevented the language from creolization.[5]

3.2 Language structure and origin

When trying to imagine where Shelta derives from it is important to focus on the things we know about their culture and lifestyle. According to their occupation as tradespeople it can be assumed that in earlier times Travellers were presumably trilingual. They must have spoken English, Irish and a form of Shelta which had probably its own grammatical system. Each of these languages had a specific role in the Travellers life and was bound to different social situations. Through constant language contact and the changing from one language to another grammatical differences made quick communication rather difficult. One could deduce from this assumption that this might be an explanation for the non-existence of Shelta syntax and no documentary evidence of an own grammatical system.[6]

When looking at the current form of Shelta this theory should be kept in mind. Shelta's vocabulary consists mostly of Irish words which have been transformed by using a number of regular changes. Macalister named eight methods of word formation or disguise in his book "The Secret Languages of Ireland" (deaspiration, denasalisation, substitution, apocope, prefixes, metathesis, reversal of syllables, complete reversal). Although there are also a few Shelta words that have not derived from Irish and whose origin is still unknown. To narrow these down the Celtic scholar Kuno Meyer has established four simple rules for the methods of disguise in Shelta: Substitution of letters, prefixing of arbitrary letters, reversal

---

[5] Alice Binchy, Irish Travellers: Culture and Ethnicity. (Belfast, W&G Baird Ldt. 1994), 144f.
[6] Alice Binchy, Travellers and their language.(Belfast, Optec, 2002) 15f.

of the word and the transposition of letters. "The existence of 'disguise' pro-
cesses in Shelta actually reflects the richness an antiquity of Shelta" (Ó hAodha
2002, 56)

Also Shelta shares Irish's basic sound system. On the other hand it takes its
syntax and grammar from English. The words take the same possessives, plu-
rals and auxiliaries as well as English verb endings. Also the language is be-
lieved to be very old because archaic words from Old Irish are used in a dis-
guised form. Moreover words seem to have been formed from pre-aspirated or
lenited Irish which could only have been taken from Irish before the rule of leni-
tion in the 12th century. Interesting is the fact that English and Irish derive from
two different branches of the Indo-European language. The former is a German-
ic language and the latter belongs to the q-Celtic languages which find their
roots in Gaelic. "The hypothesis is that the dispersion [of the Traveller society]
caused by nomadic habits has caused the language to develop as it has. In the
present system, lexicon is the ethnic marker, and grammar represents the part
of life shared with settled society." (Binchy 1994, 150)

3.4 Identity through language

*"Language is a community, language is a person, language is people, language
is a group." (An Anonymous Traveller 202, 176)*

Irish Travellers identify themselves through not only their religion, nomadism or
their traditions but mostly through their language. One could say that in the case
of the Traveller community language serves in a way as a protection. A different
language is a marker for difference and enables the Travellers to keep their cultural heritage and lifestyle to themselves. Although Shelta is not spoken when
outsiders are around, Travellers make use of it within their group to identify
themselves as a part of the community. Identity and the issue of distinction and
self-perception are essential to the understanding of Irish Travellers. They hon-
or their culture and history greatly by keeping it alive through their language.
This might be one of the reasons why Shelta has not undergone as many
changes as other languages in the same time. Holding on to the well-
established form of the language they could ensure the communication to Trav-

eller communities in different parts of the world. Though there are slight differences in vocabulary Travellers are still able to understand and communicate in
Shelta with a community from overseas.

The case of secrecy when it comes to Travellers and their language is a very
striking. Although it is not proven settled community assumes that Travellers
have always been secretive about their lives to exclude them. That might be
true to the extent that Travellers wanted to assure the existence and distinction
of their culture. Is it possible that over the last decades the importance of secrecy has evolved out of straight necessity? The more oppression and therefore
harm was done to this minority the more it felt the need to protect their cultural
heritage. Unfortunately nomadism and Shelta, the basics of a Traveller community, are part of what makes them so unaccepted, alienated and marginalized.
They have always kept their culture, religion and language to themselves – pro-
tecting it from the lack of understanding and the risk of getting lost through oppression and assimilation. Travellers themselves want to be seen as individuals
with an own identity and not as a minority within a society that shows more or
less no acceptance for the lifestyle they have chosen or rather be born in. The
problem that inevitably rises from that point is the question of future prospects
for Travellers language.

4. Conclusion

Even though there is not much proven or confirmed evidence on the origin of
neither the Irish Travellers nor their language it is most definitely an extraordi-
nary phenomenon that the culture and Shelta have survived to this day. The
fact that it is still spoken amongst Travellers and passed on from generation to
generation without almost any changes is astonishing. The central question or
as to say the biggest worry is the survival of Traveller society and its heritage.
Furthermore it is feared that they will soon surrender assimilation and be swal-
lowed up by the superior settled community. The maintenance of Shelta does
not only lie in the hands of its speakers but in the perception and acknowl-
edgement it is given by its surrounding societies. Whenever I read about Travellers and society I read about assimilation. I always wondered why that is. Why

do people try to reach sameness when the only thing anyone really wants is acceptance for who they are? – An individual with the right to express distinctiveness through culture, religion, tradition as well as language. Integration is a word I scarcely read about and unfortunately does not seem to be an opportunity when it comes to Travellers. Concerning Shelta I have to say that research shows a growth in pride of the language and a strong attitude to prevent its extinction. Whether the rationale behind this fact is driving an even bigger wedge between Irish Travellers and the settled society remains to be seen in the future. So "a greater awareness of Traveller language amongst settled people can only be beneficial to the recognition of their distinct culture and can only enhance their ongoing attempt to achieve ethnic status in an increasingly multicultural" (Ó hAodha 2002, 60) world.

5. Bibliography

M Kirk, John ; P Ó Baoill,ed.Travellers and their Language. Belfast: Optec, 2002.

Macalister, R. A. Stewart. The Secret Languages of Ireland. Cambridge: Cambridge University Press, 1937.

McCann, May ; Ó Síocháin, Séamas ; Ruane, Joseph, ed. Irish Travellers : Culture and Ethnicity. Belfast : W&G Baird Ldt., 1994.

Gmelch, George; Gmelch, Sharon Bohn. The Emergence of an Ethnic Group: The Irish Tinkers. Anthropological Quarterly [Washington D.C.] Vol. 49, No. 4, Oct. 1976: 227.